TELEGRAMS
from the PSYCH WARD
& other poems 1995-1998

by

Marc Awodey

minimal press edition
2008

"Marc Awodey writes with mesmerizing intensity. His poems are passionate displays of cadence and rhythm; swirls of drunken, expanding metaphor, all artfully choreographed within an elegant framework of stories. Telegrams from the Psych Ward resonates with one of the most original poetic voices I've encountered in years."

--Catherine A. Salmons, 1998
poet, literary critic The Boston Phoenix

Telegrams From The Psych Ward
& other poems 1995-1998

c.2008 by Marc Awodey
ISBN 978-0-615-25629-0

first minimal press edition

Telegrams from the Psych Ward

The end of Eden is a buried meadow
of gestating coal where ashen willows lash
to muse on bruised arabesques.
The listless wilderness that was once this Eden,
rings to close bouquets on we, the florid
casualties who seal a trysting place.

It is too windy to
sit in sunlight.
Saplings would go indoors
if they could.

Birds cannot manage.
No one strolls the green
this afternoon.

Cirrus words rush
as if trying to elude
    collapsing walls.

*

All that has come,
will fall from the sphere
fruits of the World
ripen sooner each year

in measures beyond
comprehension;
in measures of failed
immolation.

So many mahatmas
have been shot, treachery
silences patriots.

So many teeth are lost
in shock treatments.
Life is endless
into invisibility;
tongues are cut out,

hands become bound
despots to smother
what was barely begotten.
A good friend

once believed his brain
was in his left foot;
he almost hopped
while trying not to limp.

*

they said I was restless
in bleary eyed wakefulness
            paced past
the nurses station several

times.   I saw
them through glass
        while I paced.

*

A cool ribbon embraced my people
this morning on the grounds.
I felt it on some skin, and turned
to return to my room

4

over steel thresholds.
Signifying a direction
I pressed a soft button into
one of the elevator walls.

Last week
I washed this elevator.
Tears cleansed linoleum scuffs
on an unpredictable floor.

Accustomed now
to these surroundings
I do not weep in the elevator.
Tears seep into the ground outside.

But now
breakfast approaches.

*

Father sat seized like The Thinker
at foot of his daughter's bed.

Mother watched wretchedly alone
a few feet away from her result.

I saw them from a hallway
while returning to my room,

I accidentally looked in
in an abrupt pebble of a glance,

upon hearing fresh sobs.
Daughter remained crumpled no differently

than she had been upon her gurney
as an involuted doll

tossed into a Radio Flyer,
wheeled into a snowy room.

*

      A mess swirls.
Leafless branches
   and crimson limbs
      thicken into lukewarm ice cream.
 eyes and odors/ antiseptic despair
branches bleed
        Watchmen advance
   with fleets of dogs,
 ora pro nobis   ora pro nobis
ora pro nobis pray for us.

*

In the madder of full blooded light,
our Sun dropped a faience hood
to crucify beaten cloud banks
burnt by cinnamon, hung at night-rise
under an absinthe sky.
Seven weeping oceans multiplied
shimmering flames along
the Titan's tongue.
On sickle-shaped sand dunes
profiles darted and died,
as coasting pelicans
saw their shadows spun.

A cooling west dilates
my blistered eyes, and under
a crimson hour I'm prey to spin-

while hollow twilight guides
a virgin choir, and nihilism
thrives on jazz and Bombay gin.

Sub rosa east of Luna's jessamine,
our Sun stockpiles fuel,
for cock crow's fire.

*

Parallel stepped hills
constructed by brown ants,
and young moths living as larvae;
I saw what was seen
in a kindergarten.

These grounds are burial grounds.
Blades cast whirlpools of shadow
onto soiled fugues of heart.
Stalks of lemon-grass palpate
in sighs of circulating current.

These kernels cover reversed remains.
Seeds as loaves are split here.
Ceilings walk with a small eye.
        I have walked on this retablo
better than walking in any city.

These monuments mark empty kingdoms
below bright welters of pure,
pealing birds
balanced within hanging tree fatherlands.

I sat upon that ground
and looked low toward mixed grasses
their eyes were peppered with clover,

twigs and a university of living things
above my smoldering body.

*

The flinty constellations
of each hemisphere curl together
over hands of waxen holly.

Having misplaced Arcturus,
all I may recall is it
was rubescent and seemed nearby.

*

Beyond these yet vertical walls
small caliber locust trees
resonate in nocturnal mist.

Soon I will go home,
to rest undisturbed
upon a bed of nails
and colorful pillows.

It is strange to have no voice;
to watch clouds passing
above bricks arranged
to become architecture.

My quiet mind
has been anesthetized
to conditionally overshadow
    an Armageddon of mind
beneath these locust-

these little trees
shading an empty place.

Today is warm
in the better part of May.

*

  Overcast morning
birds are subdued.

Something will change.
genesis and bereavement will stroll
like the four legs of a prowling cat.

A jet plane spear point scraped
coldness above my temperate ribs.

An oriole inquired
   from her thin perch
and took to wing
at queer the sound of human flight.

*

now and then I reap typhoons
and heave on a stormy afternoon

my older brother quit smoking Drum
to become a Professor of Philosophy

my wife desires a speedy return
to lithium, or wherever I was

perhaps I was in a glass bottom poem
and drunk behind the steering wheel

I saw twa corbies beside a green
yearling moose, ten miles away

slipping underneath a red-tailed hawk
scanning the dozen stations, puffing

steaming serpents that arose from sea
and hissed through Port Authority-

within my routine strangulations bulge
the lashes of vulcanized effigies

and colossi are suffocated into gravel-
angry lords, why bother with me?

 -now and then I will reap typhoons
and heave into stormy afternoons

*

Let ego lap
onto untroubled shores
and hair become weft
for lea.

In time no palm
will bequeath its oil
no psyche will stream
a scion.

Let carrion nourish
a thousand scads
as sinews unbind
their lading.

Let ego lap
onto untroubled shores
and hair become weft
for lea.

*

The spell subsides.
Reticent seething
of night breath
is slowly exhaled.

Allow airless lungs
to rest awhile,
like emphysema solved.

Just awhile,
in this bed in this
hospital

for now. And later
take small sips of air
to avoid another spell.

The theoretical mechanics of healing.

In this murky quarter-
more come in walking
than go out walking.
Workers here wear sensitive gloves
of latex bled from beatific trees,
and shipped over miles of water.
All will leave eventually.
All are metamorphosed by what are
the theoretical mechanics of healing.

Some rooms contain bone saws
others contain life sustaining machines
some contain plastic bags full of robes,
and heavy boxes loaded with Styrofoam shoes.
Doors remain locked
the glass was reinforced.
Bittersweet medicines,
therapy, and death
certificates are dispensed
here with equal nonchalance
by blurry people wearing empathy
beneath their discreet, breathing masks.

*

This morning at home
first morning at home
since about Mother's Day
read poems under polished chrome
slices of Vladimir Horowitz,
as my cat enjoyed her solarium.

I took coffee
beside a tin of Top,
then read a newspaper
at six o' clock.

No ativan
assisted my sleep last night,
but soon I must concede again
to morning medications-

then I'll eat one or two
English muffins.

<u>Rain</u>

The cusp of two seasons
meandered with Venus
touching a tract of rhapsody

to ascend on generous currents
as our giant World spun onward.
Autumn approached under a rose

on the temper of divided ambitions.
Some would weather the fall.
Others would tack toward warmer climes
only to return in spring.

*

Lightning is most memorable
above cooling winds at 4 a.m.
after a stately night of violence
has unified heaven and soil.

Greensward broils,
foliage trembles over nests
in an indecisive wind.
A sickly yellow meridian

stalled over New England
to become unthinkably poised.
Settled on a secluded bank,
I praised my polished catch

of pouting small mouthed bass
while they perished, and waved
in a cache of silken pennants
on a stringer in the stream.

And on a flurry of agitated purple,
wild and heavy gusts twisted trees
last night at 3 a.m., as my headlights
crushed a viscous migration of toads.

Oily shadows tango in tremors
of humidity on scruffy patches
of graceless dust bowl. Lovers
embrace as mounds of cloud

reorganize into unlimbered fists
of pitiless cumulus thunderhead.
Daytime blisters numb skin.
Daytime bleaches fugitive dyes.

*

In a curvilinear spell
autumn reconnoitered hillsides
beneath dove clouds.

Summer was more than lustrous.
Teal threads fused beguiled moments
into an elaborate delusion
under August's decoupage.

Lemon birch leaves
and rouged maples must soon turn
under hazel forests of brittle limb,
to uphold winter's grim paradise.

*

Fading light moves west to east
to bathe a stoic neighborhood
in reams of squandered light.

And in the west is a hidden truth,
as thunderstorms caucus above my roof-
and molting birds of prey
play across sunset.

A tempest enters to baptize black
pavements adorned by old accidents
in yellow, night, and canary lines.

The traps of heaven unhinge,
and dimes of rain fall
    in escadrilles
like devils after pride,
into a bottle into a brown bag
of windless perdition.

Walking people begin to run,
and run beneath the rain, and run
before dripping houses, over bricks,
through slashes of aureate beaming-
over dissolving shadows, past
cedar shakes, pictures windows
that reflect upon the runners
in the peach flesh of vesper light.

*

Weeks of drought
claw to clutch a petty deluge;
as hope becomes a flashing ruckus
and helps a dying summer mend.

Rest as you wish to-
listening to white noise broadcast
over sidewalk slates, urban hued,
bathing under unsustained tears.

Morning rain tumbles thick
in ragged spits
onto a dappled microcosm-
it all unravels like chintzy yarn
over rumpled wooden dwellings.

These are the eggshell afternoons
that yield hours of remembrance.
Hollow downpours haul old faces
into mercurial pools of thought
caught mimicking puddled spray.

Rest as you need to, nothing
yet rattles your nine pane windows;
a speaking wind has not yet cast
rain from the eaves into your glass.
*

Exuberance flowed through flames of hair from
blasts of rain sustained in open air on sixty
miles of North America. Had this 10 a.m. been
clear jubilating music would've slung out to
scramble after a liver painted log truck.
Admiring uplands north of basalt plains, our
eyes would soon hunt jackrabbits on a rich
malpais. Overstepping polychrome we would
wonder at and mourn rectangular Mogollon
kivas exposed to the end of the twentieth
century. Postcards sent to girlfriends knowingly
untenable in Saginaw, could not recount in
pictures or dashed off words widening worlds.
Bivouacked within mummy bags beside
momentary landscapes dotted in hogans and
Quonset huts; ratatat constellations will run for
360 degrees around a campfire's helix of

aspiring embers. But no one sails on
cloudbursts. Rain hissed. A mahogany guitar
persevered beneath billows of ragged blue
poncho. Ends of cloth waved in spray atomized
over spinning tires. The tires painted serpents
onto a crumbling, frost heaved turnpike.

*

The first snow angels have clambered
from mud to get on to school
in radiant coats and black galoshes.

The Earth is baklava, its cloudy
rafters are Milton's eyes.
A wheelbarrow of bric-a-brac

crosses decadent streams
Worms were knotted into leafy tufts
kneaded into Monday's sidewalk stains

by a pack of inoculated children
-a tad guilty, a tad innocent.
Luminous hydras ripple on my wall

as liquid hailstones cuff steaming
glass; a cotton quilt embalms my body
to rest on a sagging sofa.

Reflections look heavenward
from an archipelago of puddles,
hundredweights of aphids cluster

on the bark of each ticklish branch.
Traffic signs stab the avenue's
green belt- honorable Senators

stand above a fountainhead
of rotting twigs. To me, falling
is to fall and be pounced upon

by lurid automobiles.
The artery below is rich
with lurid automobiles.

*

Leaves mew
in small and gentle voices
as pregnant milkweed,
and cottonwood whiskers

symmetrically loiter
in sunlight. Exposed seeds
polished before exhales
are offered to regenerate

acid burned forests.
My son once heard me
muttering to no one
about a place of warm wind.

Ascending sounds
of morning unfold as twilight's
embroidered train atrophies
over the fog drugged Adirondacks.

Swarming raindrops
rattle on my sash.
Beyond dripping clapboards
I hear October's last finch.

*

At flood stage the river
quit its timeworn bends.
Trees became flotillas torn
to writhe along the river's brim.

Under yesterday's rolling bolt
of amassed rain, slouched hills
endured the river's hypocrisy.
Only stone hindered tributaries.

Towns upstream were washed over.
Our intervale was washed over.
Em-browned water beat through
afternoon into a weedy midnight

and almost into stands of dawn.
A stone faced sun sealed in agar
now smirks over hung over water.

*

A red taffeta umbrella
hid a slim pedestrian
from rain,
and mist
around unbudded box elders
on the first day of spring.

Dawn was dim,
lavender and the pear
trees stood tall as straw men
while naked gusts and sleeting
ice diffused my light
on the last day of November.

We Never Knew the Sea

As small travelers subject to heavy clouds,
we silently sought the edge of our continent.
We vaporized near breakwaters as our paths
met icebergs warming under quilts of ocean.
I fell on my knees, and began sculpting sand
as two fair women wandered far out-of-the-way
to greet an easterly wind.

*horizons

On luminous ocean and salt water;
on inland sea and elegant foam;
on reclining savanna of spilling grass;
and interminable fields of ice,
horizons cannot change character.

Variegated grounds must meet
to overlap clear, broken or tumbling
firmament. Titans graciously embrace
as a father and mother do.

The colors of the land are in the clouds.
Cloudy colors are outstretched over land.
Our evening tide is lavender,
mummy is the morning sky.   Split
is the vision of razor wire that hems
us into a living world each hour;
below a holed cosmos,
above groaning bedrock.

I have yet to be among the clouds,
I am yet to be devoured by umber peat.

*our empty sea

Under our empty sea
an indigo world exists
as a once familiar voice
now far beyond recollection,
and over trench, plateau, barrow
of cloudy schist.
On the tossing desert continuum resides
a pacific mind, and in each ocean mind
there are dreams of drying soil.

Solitary whales ponder the odds
of an earthen surface
laying above heaven's lucid touch
of rolling amethyst.
In pencil thin ends
of falling daylight beams
and over trench, plateau,
barrow of cloudy schist;
wrinkled pods of philosophers
sing to theorize
of crossing high ocean
under clouds of billowed sail.

We may follow the smooth descent
of necklaced emperor penguins
from high above heaven's lucid touch
of rolling amethyst,
into the open jaws of unimpressed
killer whales
who antiphon on ocean floor
the prayers of killer whales.

Do not mourn the passing of sea creatures
into sustenance, while crossing
high ocean under clouds of billowed sail-
Of that unwholesome meat,
tossed red into sponginess
will arise an unknown landscape
undreamt of.
And forever anon and forever again
dancing penguin must
harmonize with the hungry souls
who antiphon on ocean floor
the prayers of killer whales.

*intermezzo

Plum is the voice of evensong
intermezzo over unsung phrases of day;
when septet tunes and turns a page

then stage belongs to a lone nocturne
intermezzo over unsung phrases of day.
Silence is briefly an inwrought song;

then stage belongs to a lone nocturne
sung by birds who have nested and gone.
Silence is briefly an inwrought song

as played by oboes that have no reed,
sung by birds who have nested and gone
on declining stars in rising dawn;

as played by oboes that have no reed.
When septet tunes and turns a page
on declining stars in rising dawn
plum is the voice of evensong.

*

While posed as sailing angels
we are tattooed on high,
though in our breaking epiphany
skyscrapers must pale
to know the ballast stones
of sunken merchantmen
will arise on unknown landscapes,
undreamt of.

Uncaring flukes concentrate
to ply compassionless brine
for in each ocean mind
there are dreams of drying soil-
fashion scrimshaw as your vessel
rides on mumbling heaves,
though in our breaking epiphany
skyscrapers must pale.

Let terra incognito
dissolve in faultless sea
for under our empty sea
an indigo world exists.

*

They scooped their beds where a silver river
wrinkled and rose to raft the fry that failed,
over embryos, and last year's leaves.
I followed the arcs of salmon,
and saw them spawn on gravel gems;
costumed in false red jaws.
They scooped their beds where a silver river
wrinkled and rose to raft the fry that failed,
over embryos, and last year's leaves.

*harbor

We knew a seemingly endless thread
of peppery beach and beach grass,
we watched an azure haze enfold horizon-
but we never knew the sea.

What we spoke of is sincerely lost
though could shoreline be refound
the sound of sounding lighthouse
would not acquiesce to variance
beyond an ashen, inevitable sound.

If echoes could once more disperse
all shades of ghost below
an empty western field-
sandpipers would not conjure
fewer risks.
Frail rows of curling waves would break
in strains that do not murmur any less;
yet your sound would not resound a sea-
  for we never knew the sea.

Every Winter, Every Spring

Jesus wept.
So you have wept
while writing poems and letters,
    so too have you wept
while understanding moments past.
You have held your deciduous leaf
and seen it turn within the hand-
    there is no shame in that.
And anyway, when you are gone
so too will be your secrets passed.

    Good day-
I will be an open berth
for what has gone before
and do no harm by doing so
and weep, and weep, and weep,
      and weep
mid all the sweetness that I know;
for in that shredded sanctum idles
every bleating trauma of the soul.

I'll nourish what has gone before
    and welcome what is sure to be-
for when my thirteenth chime has tolled,
all of this untold history, poetry, love
    apprehensive- unbelieved;
will meet the drifter of the night
who cracks dream tumblers
to become a thief.

*

Unwatchful lanterns raise without light
chambers where neighbors may nevermore
speak, and the fences that surround amnesia.

In summer an emerald canopy closed
to conceal village tongues and old dialects,
in silent yards measuring a ruinous night

and leaves bound to fall like wings
from grace to mingle with newspaper,
books, and grass-

in silent yards measuring a ruinous night
and chambers where neighbors
may nevermore speak

under unwatchful lanterns
that raise without light
the fences that surround my amnesia.

*

Apple pickers
wear straw hats
in the orange
glare
of western Michigan.
They stand
on wooden ladders
and work in rows
of well kept trees
as iridescent flies
dance, involuting
on the broken
branching rhythms
of green
and ruffled
pointed leaves.

We twisted thousands
of fibrous stems
to spot pick
an good hard crop
of Macintosh, red
and golden delicious.
We balanced
canvas strapped
buckets
of bushels
across ranging shoulders
and took
jaunty pains
to avoid bruising
the boss's crop.

*

In a mumbling ravine that sags
beside an elbow that bends
into a gray river-
the tangled flesh of fiddleheads
covers accrued litter;
from tin to broken glass,
and brambles on the floor
of my mumbling ravine.

I have searched for antique bottles
but never found one intact.
Trees split by storms make holes
of sky in contrapuntal patterns
of light and wet and furious leaves
over the footprints of fallen trees.
The holes are refilled every year,
by angled trunks, and splintered bones.

*

Ephemeral
on the seventh of May
agile on imperceptible niches,
unfurled by whispers
of new born air
and the petals of sparse seconds-

she laughed
while juxtaposing perennials
and markings of mustard and jade
that lit camouflage on flickering wings.

Neither monarch nor moth,
nor any other prosaic species-
a singular piece of confetti
fancied only to ascend, and so
she crawled out of a chrysalid womb
at first no larger than the wrinkled thumb
of a premature child.

Mute to all but her own rare species
animation uncurled to crisscross
my sad wisdom and myriad other fields
of vision- she was a psaltry string
to orthodox eyes well versed
in nothingness
beyond my narrow hedge; and away
to dicker with picayune currents of air,
she would land on one more pistillate blast
of many suspended hues.

*

Song birds preen themselves
in the heart of a yellow pine

shielded from the pearly scraps
of breeze that pass for sacred song.

A giant revealed by needles of pine;
it felt no axe sixty years ago,

it was not rolled into the river
like a stone, beside husky brothers

when this tract was cleared
and these little balloon framed houses

were framed by quarter sawn beams
floated down from Canada.

It drinks from a spring fed aquifer.
It looks heaven in the eye.

It bends in no season.
Though perfectly high

enough for lightning's play,
no lightning has touched it.

It stands alone in the old quarter
of a sloping city. A wooden house

slumps nearby in solitude
waiting to collapse-
a toppled waffle cone, full of ants.

*
Strange voiced animals argue,
    and gesture

every evening-
they argue over precedence,
and rank
and litter tossed in,
in plastic bags
from passing automobiles
off the avenue; and half hot dogs
in paper, unspilled beer bottles
and peanut butter jars-
from the sidewalk on the rim,
 and from under my own
bungee wrapped
garbage cans with half-cocked
Rubbermaid lids.

The voices subside each winter
when the river is frozen
and five feet of snow
compresses into its self
on the sagging floor
of my mumbling ravine.

*

A fractured man is posed
on crumbling stairs
above a lawn
tinted by Monday's shade-
he hears a yellow jacket
buzzing there, like a wire
to grow vexatious music
on verdigris blades.
Knotting the tired hands
of his truant life -
mocked to tears
by dry and purposeful

insect lives,
where plenty and contentment
rattle ripe-
no vagrant drones
can last within a hive.
Indigo butter knives play
on stirring grass
his marrow is gooey,
inert and ivory black
he smokes a cigarette says-
"this will pass"
a muttering breeze then
ripples over his back;
and likewise realized
in ancient stings of bee,
   and bee metaphors, wax
frenzies under hazes
yet unappeased.

*

Please speak of birth
for a change-
I heard the airy utterances
of a crested cardinal shielded
under foliage today.

Its speech was berry red.
Its ribbon of whistling streamed
over triangles of morning shade
signaling to a lover perhaps
above layers of whispering leaves.

I did not see its scarlet
but I heard its succulent color
and timbre in my complicated wood

clear over the staccato Babel
of less luminous birds.

All of the nesting races
dangled in arboreal mobiles
squirming full of hatchling mouths
delicately beaked and tongued,
woven shrewdly together under songs.

*

Today the sky is sapphire gin,
so I weigh the pear trees
we have cultivated
in our little plot.

They both require sunbeams
they were both once rousing sprigs
they seem to survive every winter;

one of them balances uprightly
somewhere in the South,
while the other one bends tenuously
to become a constant worry.

Poetry of Place

1. Ruin

Carts of wool were brought in
to acquire eagles and horse blankets.
Men in straw hats spoke to men in silk.

Oxen snorted under daylight.
The lissome fingers of mill girls
danced over ironhanded machines.

Fibers in light beams rose
over wailing shuttles and chains.
An oak wheel groaned.

Reflections run along the river;
and the river's brooding skin.
In spalling courses of kiln brick

melting upon well faced blocks,
the masonry of lost trades
at this place disintegrates

under a decade's afternoon,
transfigured into memory
and a scab of ruddy ruin.

2. A Majestic Girl

Night beyond seeing is history.
Gleaming light bulbs are driven by
watery things destroyed inside

of turbines spun by crushed
rivers and woods. Science

33

transmutes the exhales of fishes

into cotton bolls of heat.
Unmoving hills of waiting fuel
sleep beside our power station.

Wood chips molder into fungi
rich kindling, these were once
a northern forest.

Axe handles of ash
keep in mind lusty trespasses,
for each tree of moody canopy

is an unwitting marker
of centuries. Each stands on age
uniquely in a family of ages

many rings older than any frail
person lost leaning on a walnut
cane in dignified remembrance

who quietly folds her hands
in an immaterial town. Here
are the grandchildren of slaves.

They age in steely forbearance.
Some of them have fought
in foreign wars. Others were once

working children baptized
by these mills. They whisper
Quebecois lullabies and remember.

Some were paid in silver coin
at Christmas. Liberty was then
portrayed as a majestic girl.

Some were paid from perfumed
purses in gold. Upon these coins
were Indian heads. Some here are

descended from ironsmiths
who forged repeating rifles
from raw materials, and manacles

to be shipped in prodigious
Yankee quantities to be worn
by the fore mothers of our

Southern émigrés. Some rest
and wait in quiet convalescence.
All rest and wait

regardless of age
under the psyche of another
morning's broken yoke.

3. The Winooski Bridge

In sunken tattoos and diesel smoke
heavy orange machines do heavy work

ripping iron out of concrete clouds,
while hardhats emanate daylight.

The Winooski bridge is being restored.
Unplanned for tons of cramped modernity

have bruised its 1928 spine and ribs.
Workers are bound to engineers

dressed in working clothes; harnessed
to dangle from i-beams they swarm

over, and under steel triangles.
Scratching signatures into girders

they do overlook the bits of asphalt
that do inevitably fall and sink
while breaking out old pavements.

One From Four

1. flower day

On Flower Day exiles remember
the dead, with milk
and flowers placed on standing stones.
This Land of the Grandmother
is like any unchosen land.

Prodigal deposits of sleeping minerals
wait to be taken from under feet.
Threadbare prairies marked by cairns
veil snake holes from needles of rain.

They who once knew no borders
now edge a well defined emptiness,
for only unturned fields were esteemed
by the parents preserved below
these memorials bearing English

translations of names
recent generations
would find hard to pronounce.

2. watchers

Gaping spirits watch
through mica windows at Acoma.
Some have matted hair,

curled finger nails.
Some still have lips,
and eye lids.

They watch water carriers
zigzagging up the mesa trail.
They see coffee pots, medicine

bottles a few inches tall.
They watch children, old women
burnishing ceramics,

young men circling want ads,
brides bathing,
old uncles playing cards,

house cats lost in the hunt.
They see vapor trails discarded
by intercontinental flights.

Some have no right hands
or left feet. All were once
heaving loaves of birth.

Watching is all they can do.

3. Cahokia

When people
were allowed to believe the World
had come to an end
centuries before William Henry Harrison,
no East St. Louis was dreamt of
on virulent prairies near Cahokia.

We may today only pretend to taste
russet formulations of remedy,
and admire the elegant emissaries
dispatched by Lord Thirteen Rabbit.

We may surmise the rustle of bright cloaks
woven from New World feathers, the murmurs
and jubes, of pious farm families adoring
virgin demigoddesses tied in a row.

We admire the man made mountain
once crowned by temple zenith;
while searching above our interstate,
for signs of the Mississippi.

We can try to reconstruct emotions,
into chants and prayers that whisper
apologies addressed to ancestors-

postmarked via archaeology
from the shoulder of last day
of the World.

4. dried dust

At the thin edge of the wedge
in an unconscious savanna
encircling flowers and sly creation,

male and female once walked a wadi
a few hours before it was interred
by an eruption of volcanic ash.

The grace of a sanguine deity
may soon unravel our mysteries
under an uncovered scrub brush plain
where fossilized footprints
in dried dust remain.

Halieutica

1. Catching conspicuous emptiness

My intimates; heron and loon
were worthier than me
at first light.

Heron's stilts poled him
over fast water.
Loon fell into the alizarin hours

of her prey.
Heron ascended on overwhelming wings

toward farther parts of the stream.
Loon glanced above
water's stretched surface,

to dive and dive again at dilatory
                    sunfish.

Catching conspicuous emptiness,
I cast monofilament into morning wind
beside sunlit hills of ebbing foam.

2. A Small Dance

They danced a small jig
in the foiled box,
warming below a sixty watt bulb.

Aping an impolite divinity,
I scooped squirming handfuls.
With the delicacy of glass animals,

they (nevertheless) attempted escape
by crawling up the cruelly waxed sides
of my sawed off milk carton.

Juice ran over futilely kicking legs and
segmented thoraxes.
Hooked in a tiny crackle;

head on a barb like regicide,
they gloriously splayed their inner-most
        wings
and buoyantly danced
once more before they gasped
and turned to sink.

3. Fish are an arduous catch

With January's thirst unquenched
silted streams were stillborn in spring.
Our lake has become sour and low.

Gulls organize on each parking lot
into groups of anxious, chalky toys
squawking louder than in last summer.

When fish are an arduous catch
beaks and feet adapt to collect
the filthy lucre of crumbs and fries

that is scattered about our fringes.
Arrayed as stalking martinets they
also snatch and spit bent cigarettes

a priori barnstorming off
like a wheeling flying circus,
 farther away from Lake Champlain.

Quebec

Winter snows accumulate on
the humus of the Plains of Abraham,
to bury hills once tinted claret
as night kneels over rundown elegies
drawn from barrels of angry grape.

Maple trees subsist upon
the humus of the Plains of Abraham.
Acrid airs once wreathed colors
as night knelt over rundown men
untended on the scavenged grounds.

*

From turned furrows
of dusky field, turkey vultures
arose deliberately
in a broad winged flock of three
arced to eulogize one more life
passed beneath a bristled hogback.

And the wind is cold,
and cold had been a June drizzle.
Leathery mud relaxes quenched
below a film of slow fermentation.

A bed of fallow deer,
sculpted around decomposition,
has been ritually cleansed
by them, the satisfied men
who spiral upward
in molting frock coats.
Minding curls of air
they nodded bald heads

to balance the spaces within
their trinity, and reclaim
a tall pulpit from whence
they would soon circle again.

*

My annihilated house
heaped into jaws of cellar; was limed
by itinerant clouds on a Saturday morn.

Snow rested here midst black cornices,
residing in domes on shriveled diaries,
consigned to flame on a Friday night.
Pale cheek bones histrionically rose
to process eastwardly for seppuku
and over ocean they made their peace

on a Sunday faraway from what is buried
here beyond the conception
of Friday's candle-light.

*

All crumpled into jejune quadrilles
without spry girls, punch, or fiddlers.
They followed a swift medicine
as boards of pine met bone saw teeth.
They followed like brave gentlemen,
their Kings.

*

A freight train gestured from faraway
over tatters of freezing sunset.
Homes and cars in this perplexing valley
have become grounded reminders of stars.

Let me be the first to fall into sleep
under linen November bedclothes,
for I have seen too much today
to hope to gaze into livid evening.

Each century is oppressively chimerical;
and gaudiness is mistaken for radiance.
I am a son among a million bewildered sons
who haunt quiet, productive wastelands.

Let me be the first to fall into sleep
for I have seen too much today.

*

Montcalm and Wolfe coolly followed
above grenadiers past Montmorency,
and a homespun field of uniforms worn
on conscripts born within New France.

*

The tyranny of passage
is toned by resignation.
Unintended detours
have become seductive.
Scarves unravel into day
passing into night.
Tragedian constellations
above white noise conceal
dull ruminations, and hushed
degrees of sulky glaciation.
Brightened breaths puff and bloom
braced by white aurora strewn
from the chimneys of flesh and blood
hamlets under waves of sackcloth hills.

Riddles echo in my bundled head;
(beckoning the frozen dead)
car lights, street lights toss
ill fated shades over the avenue.
Secrecy illumines streaming steps.
Illusive landmarks shepherd me home.

*asylum:

Let us admire the misted machicolation
of an afternoon fallen to embrace our city of
Quebec.

Last night's squall has fallen
toward the Atlantic ocean.
Continuations of dust descend
upon the grace of morning.

Now and then a fiery furnace
cools in voluminous thaws
such as this.
Conciliated winds mutter as creamy
madrigals caress transient harmonies.

Many an iota of skin has lilted
in lucency over my flights of stair.
A house is obliged to shelter all
who may believe they need sheltering.

No one can say,
or conceive of what
the next revolution may bring.

Shibboleth

*

In a side yard garden orchids thrive,
some are mauve and some are white.

A captive sun smiles on fruitful lives
where the fruit of flowers is color.

Belladonna veins wrap garden gate;
who can whisper the shibboleth of a name?

Finches' beaks are sharp as knives
their shrill notes pierce warm days with ease.

The fruit of song birds
is inarticulate flight.

*

Morning is becoming electrokinetic again
over lone passions- life, expiration.

Cock crow calls forth addle-brained streams
over flattened grasses gone yellow,

gone brown, once green.
Satellites sleep juxtaposed

unobservable stars
scattered under a rib cage cradle

that is our luminous east.
In thorny shrubs finches chatter

like bowl backed mandolins
in groups of two and three, unseen

while cock crow calls forth empty streams
of warm and lucid wind.

*

Between the crestfallen quivers of
a few barnacled leaves; each noun

echoes as one incarnation of creation.
Umber autumn adjusts her reins

around our empty eyed sun.
        -Vishnu-

slashes, whips, rides roughshod upon
the golden hoard of a compromised Khan.

*

When light falls far from any prying witness,
night's lofty peroration is solely addressed

to the mighty ears of nervy bats.
As finches' beaks glint sharp as knives

secreted under wooden fingers of nest,
no one may see jade stars progress

in flocks of self-absorbed zodiacs.
When light falls like a stricken jet

beyond the hopes of shocked witnesses
our earth beclouds into a mindless onyx

crippled by hints of unknowable things.
No one may see jade stars progress.

*

Blind
yet without bat ears in my catastrophes,

knowing that by a blind moon
heaven is lavishly blessed, sensing

that she is as blind as a book
I read and write in darkness

as miles of living cloud engulf
my shrinking circle of sky.

*

In imitation of amourosis, belladonna
vines coil garden's gate

without observing inconveniences
that do and must divide day and night.

Turning in her faithful white-
the eyes of our simple-hearted moon.

Each sun smiles on fruitful lives,
planets reconnoiter nine automatic dawns.

Engraved on the backs of Christian names
borne on ten thousand accents, cacophonous

with names are terms that quantify
and divide the remembered, the lost,
the unplaced and almost forgotten names.

*

A poet's morning stretches
into flagging colors along the west.

Satellites sleep juxtaposed
unobservable stars.

The satellite pearl is uncomposed
in her slumbering heap.

She smiles- well aware, (well asleep)
to know which words will dissipate

as the grandiloquent planets
glisten under nine automatic dawns.

*

Finches' beaks are sharp as knives
their shrill notes pierce warm days with ease.

The fruit of song birds is inarticulate flight.
The fruit of flowers is faded color.

Between the crestfallen quivers of
a few red, barnacled leaves- who will whisper

the shibboleth of my name
gone yellow, gone brown, once green?

Wednesday

Here I launched my silver fleet-
but not to fight divine puppeteers
where our sun falters on her guarded face,
though perhaps my devotion should have gone.
But I was never one to war
and I was never one to risk
a better passion passing years encamped
on iron beaches or near gently rising plains.

*

Souvenirs of Wednesday remain
untouched by a moment's mind
though pockets have grown heavy
after Tuesday's withering hail
spoke in a stone fusillade.

A murder of crows arose over lea
everyday thoughts were carried by wings,
to drift like oil on an empty sea.
Citizens of ocean, land, and ether
desperately practice private arts
as if each returning day
were a ruby arched Redeemer.

Heads wear silver time pieces
sowing momentous ticks and tocks,
to cherish aimless rays abandoned
by the sun's Apollonian palm.

*

   While Paris lives I am fated to resist
under granite hills beside a calmer sea,
as disassembled planks and spars recall

what grand intention had them roughly hewn
before they knew this house of quiet memory.
Brown coal now warms this wooden house-
and sealed within a furnace heart persists
an hidden immolation to be ever ill contained.

*

I dig in my coat for matches
an old familiarity with roots in soil
places blooms against the palms
like vermilion verisimilitudes.
I'll exhaust weeks of solitude,
trying to survive the ninth month.
I'll scrape sulfur across the marl-
as nude skies move knowingly
without being noticed from earth.

Per chance seeds will germinate
on Thursday or perhaps Friday.
Per chance upon a nameless day
as a tier of top-soil conceals
tenements of clay.

But Wednesday next will surly reap
from beds of leveled minds;
gourds, root crops, grains, legumes,
and fleshy vegetables left to rot
under the veins of twisted vines.
*
 And I will furl my sails again in every spring
that grows more white as each precedes my fall,
to fall on hollow tocsin bells where fall
the stars that should have guided me to Ilium.
And in grim faith I'll surly stand beside
the bed where I have died

that ought have been a bloody shield perhaps,
to raise a barren hand and ask with Homer's
empty eyes- Aphrodite, does Paris still live?

*

Mist fused sky and water
over waters freed from waxen ice.

as memory in a dry mouth
kicked at loosened chains.

Thoughts turned outward
so too blooming Christmas cacti.

Rumpled people disinterred
glaring to-do lists and lingered

wrapped in balmy things;
ascendant naiads of spring,

spawning walleye, precious sturgeon.
Rainbow trout in ponds as inky
as an inch of wormwood tea.

But cirrocumulus curls appeared
to snarl a trompe l'oeil heaven.

Baroque, broken cherubs froze
as umber trees sprouted aureoles

and northerly skies writhed
like horses in electrum filigree.

El Nino once blessed Boston;
while we knew sleep paralysis,

and diamonds fell before February
parallel unexplored illusions.

One Brief Man: a poem in three dimensions

*[Degradation dances on urban clouds as the
description of another hour wrinkles under the
present tense. Enter MAN & CHORUS all
dressed in street clothes. CHORUS is tied up
like a chain gang, gender, ethnicity unimportant.
MAN speaks with expansive gestures]:*

Sweet air wreaths to crown this hill
transcending cast concrete grotesques,
no smokestack plume or fume can wound
my Mind's mirage, delicate as it is.

Inhale these unfledged chlorophylls
looming from path to garden's gate;
oil rainbows dissipate as spilled
near the lowly black and canary lines
that bless our Northeast avenue.
From tall coteries of philosophers
to sexton tended grounds
my meadow simply mellows into slough.

CHORUS: Let us shout,
from free libraries to ask why.
Why may no harvest thrive on salted fields?

MAN: Let us re-ingest ingested seeds
now broadcast from on high
by the Gordian gut of a hermit thrush.

And perhaps with equal justice
we can relish the boiling jams,
meads, and anisette liqueurs,
that earthbound starlings also knew?

Perhaps they may be gathered into one
amalgamated Brunelleschi seed,
put up in jars and sealed with paraffin?
Perhaps they must be counted on
to breed in slippery meadows
under blue and wrinkled elbows
that root in gnarled orchards
bound to mellow into slough?

CHORUS: Rejuvenated beyond a fear of being;
spread by one of several fluted blades...

MAN: I have NOT ascended here to sing
with all the mindless husks of grain
nor truly storm in jumbled tongues
an old time, patriarchal,
'neath a loop of rattling serpent
jubilee tonight!

CHORUS: Praise be to GOD!
[then murmuring, like a mercurial brook]
Blither Blather Blither Bleed...
Blither Blather Blither Bleed...
Blither Blather Blither Bleed...

MAN: Bejeweled shadows seep Chinese ink
through my paper portrait
underneath a feral Moon,
becoming evermore exquisite
more than any proof-like coin;
as gangs of ancient facets dug
from blue earth archipelagos
slog to shove wheelbarrows full
with pyramids full of fruit withdrawn

from fuchsia meadows under red delicious
branches wherein broad epaulets just begin
to touch the sweat stained petals stuck to
greasy orchids as they steam on mantis arms.

 Hoisted, I twist
on a shaky trapeze
of humming liquid apostrophes
called forth to woo domed ladybugs;
though certain my predictions
are unheeded as they mellow into slough-

[in agony] Forgive my woeful retreat
from your lamentable city.

CHORUS [slyly]: Ah, but...if one brief man
can survive his own noxious juice
to inhale the ounces of hazy perfume
that seem to have sprung
from unfledged chlorophyll-

*[45 seconds pass in silence, like ghosts, as MAN
walks in a circular perambulation totally self-
absorbed.]*

MAN: then all my freezing exhaled air demands
that all these berries,
spit and spread,
corkscrew in well-born holidays
 to be placed in state
within an all-encircling wreath.
 For each of my more savory treats
may only bloom where there resides
the drunk and orphaned meadows
under orchards, born to mellow into slough.

This Lake has no Name

Twenty thousand souls
swell beneath these waves
each whitecap is a headstone,
each billow is a grave.

With shoulders drenched by cannonballs
men fought to give you their name-
their names now lay beside sturgeon,
and spars that were charred by flame
their beards are tangled in milfoil
their eyes stare into green, and we
now praise your luster, your glimmer, your hills
without asking for your name.

We did not dream above your petrified whales,
while sawing trees and nailing ash to cross
your inland sea. We slipped our ships around
Cumberland head- such was the northern dream,
to round Valcour, the Four Brothers,
and ultimately Ticonderoga.

The men of the west were painted and brave
they chose their friends based on their enemies,
the men of the east were painted and brave
they chose their enemies based on their enemies-
Algonquin, Iroquois, English, French,
Black American, Quebecois,
White American, Canadian,
 all based their enemies upon themselves,
and fought to give you their names.

We say the cormorants have invaded,
while you recall when well bred sheep

and the potash trade denuded an old growth
watershed. You dislike tasting paper pulp-
 so enter clandestine zebra mussels.

Twenty thousand souls
swell beneath these waves
each whitecap is a headstone,
each billow is a grave.

Women walk alone on brick beaches, bricks
from a wreck that foundered in your storm.
Ice fishermen pull steaming trout from your
body and grand children stand
 on ripples of sand, while your whispers wrap
their ankles in sunlight-
but we do not know your name.

Granite hills and crumbling fortresses
embrace the new leviathan,
as puffing poets praise themselves, and the rich
their charitable contributions to you.

Your waters are the blood of glaciers
your gar the serrated spawn of monsters
we serve at your pleasure, you are not of us
    -and Samuel de Champlain is dust-
while murmuring souls turn in your waves
to blossom and curl and uncurl
like fiddleheads in May, like tears
in a beard, like a baby's tongue-
innocent of words;
and only they, and only melting bones can know
the shibboleth of your true name.

Twenty thousand souls
swell beneath these waves
each whitecap is a headstone,
each billow is a grave.

<u>Work like the Devil</u>:
*as a nothingness of human hand embraces inner
psalms*

Tall upon fiber
are chopper and chopped,
in phase one of -how to spin
pink candy.

Out among hills of humid stubble,
under a hungry sun,
double edged saints glisten
lacerate, and cut cane.

Dark backs sway and bend
to lift their troubled bundles-
in the name of starving children
visiting elephantine circuses,

state fairs, carnivals,
and birthday parties everywhere.

*

A turquoise 20mg.
slouched inside
my sweltering blue
Chrysler, reactions
shut off one by one.

Workers, men
take their noontime meals
out of foil bags
and bright brown bottles.

Dream they would dream
if time allowed of *God*
knows what in this situation.

Scalps slump down
under vinyl atmospheric
conditions.
Limply lounging

in supermarket parking lots,
Procrustean rows
of expressionless eyes
steal furtive naps under
sheets of gleaming safety glass.

Let us,
   imitate
   turtle eggs
   beneath sand
and hope the most delicious
will question nothing.

*

I spin and spin
but leave no thread
riding the world
and the world is spun
by different men
who weave with guile
and glue,

I spin in reckless
nothingness,
with nothing fair
to do

my works plumb
the ugliness
of what a man goes through.

When lost to spin
and twist and spin
while wholly unable
to comprehend
what any man should do.
The wind of breath
falls closer toward
sleek blades
of morning dew,
meek shimmering breaths
blown through
a mustache
and lips to mingle
with morning dew.

*

Today i pulled out one of my teeth
        just thinking
about the old men reading
their poems   at my house
 last night

all reverent, awaiting waves
exchanging memories
comparing prisons
        clandestine moves
in images all
  reeking
of
      Merwin-

*

There are devils poised
on every leaf. Today's vaporous crux
is not so benign and heavenly

that an antidote for old whirligigs
can be unencrypted to face afternoon.
Waters prosper below sea eagles

stylistically similar to sweeping
Olympic swimmers in ash-blond sky.
These billows are not a wilderness yet

but they do approach the tidewater
and wash over somber boroughs where
flaxen flames of rooftop loll unaware

of the petty Golgothas sculpted
thereunder.
No lofty peace

can disseminate seedlings over bedrock.
No smoldering peace may rise from this
as solitary Atlases lug their gist;

each amassed burden lashed and bound
is bound to someday bend and slip
slowly onto milky eyes

to become rosettes
laconic and dry.

Form and Emptiness

This Monday is quiet as moonlight reflects upon
the faces of uncovered leaves. A thin breeze
loosens my skin over the flannel of a winding
sheet. My mind is filled with pantoums- dog
eared books, misplaced sources. A bedside lamp
clicks on again to have a smoke, a glass of
water; and stroll among the unborn ghosts.

   While beds in my garden are muddy and raw
the salt of the city does its work-
   January dissolves in an untold thaw
amid pressed grasses, snows withdraw
from a face bruised by cold winter's work.
   While beds in my garden are muddy and raw,
twisting through gutters, a long cat's paw
fills storm sewer with tinsel and murk,
   January dissolves in an untold thaw
to reveal pressed grasses of textured straw.
 as kigh over Canada snowstorms lurk.
   While beds in my garden are muddy and raw;
hydrangeas shriveled into a frozen claw
hold proof of autumn's red handiwork.
   January dissolves in an untold thaw
that my unfledged winter never foresaw;
deranged bluffs drift into solitary smirks
of jagged ice incisor on a grizzled blue jaw
   as January dissolved in an untold thaw

*

Returning from a euchre game
last night on a spiraling path,
my grove was purple
and the old scent of burning
pitch followed past warming cottages.

Each step on the gravelly way
resounded in unalterable grittiness.
Each was heavier than the jumpy steps
of childhood
tossed onto opposite gravel.
Each was heavier
than sandal steps
once laid down cautiously
beside sprightly, teasing footprints.
And each was heavier than the leather
soled steps of middle age.

An invisible formation of geese
bleated in navigation between stars
and the tangled shoulders
of leafless trees.

*

From gentle reminiscences songs undiscussed
descend-
how long in remembrance, must mountain dust
descend?

Fireflies relax entrapped by streams of morning
light-
children watch a gathering swarm's empty lust
descend.

Stares grow wide outside a vanished, vacant
church
as effervescent flowers of black emerald dust
descend.

Ping, ping, on a high old bronze bell locust roll;

of Damascus, brutish Janissaries forever must
descend.

Beside muted gutturals praying "inherit the
Earth"
a broken girl weeps in a cave- blood and rust
descend.

From Beirut, to New Orleans, and Detroit into
old age;
inarticulate immigrants trust the unjust must
descend.

Shy under slabs of memory, her oak Victrola
sings-
a robust voice, an oud, and songs of exodus
descend.

*

Two phantom boys leapt off a crescent dune
in twin elliptic long jumps arcing shore,
where shadows played on cleaving crests of
grass, scattered beneath prodigal moments
of rest in twin elliptic long jumps arcing shore.

From scalloped waves where sandy fountains
bloomed, scattered under prodigal moments
of rest- seagulls cried with shouts of joy that
soared from scalloped waves where sandy
fountains bloomed, to rise like diamond chips
on rippling backs.

Seagulls cried with shouts of joy that soared,
to dye electric blue the horizon west
and rise like diamond chips on rippling backs-

in fixed remembrance drifting over noon

They flew off every broken bluff before,
in fixed remembrance drifting over noon
a polished summer's day was left to pass.
They flew off every broken bluff before,
in swaggers 'round whose leaps alighted best
a polished summer's day was left to pass
where shadows played on cleaving crests of
grass, in swaggers 'round whose leaps
    alighted best.

Two phantom boys leapt off a crescent dune-
    one of those boys became bearded man;
    the other child is vaulted in the sand.

The Conversation

You sketched me
at the coffee house,
we absently spoke of drawing
and literature.
I took exception to the manner
in which you drew hands,
I said-
"you make them look like machines."
Citing Ingres, I plotted a continuous line.

You agreed.

Critically eying the unfledged birds
who hesitated near decorative book stacks,
I muttered a condescending remark
about nose rings, poetry, and tattoos.
But you refused to objectify
or malign, saying-
"such is the nature
of this establishment, and of youth."

I agreed.

We nodded heads
and judiciously stroked Socratic beards
as the artifice of conversation
strolled for awhile longer,
into longer pauses

over a couple of dollars worth
of cooling Ethiopian Harari.

Memoria

When a D-day dawn
of dandelion parachutes
crossed freshly sodded lawns,
and cat tail torches danced with us
around wooded hearted ravines
the harp strings of our bicycle wheels,
whirred from clothspined aces
and sighed like flurries of Zuider Zee
windmills as we patrolled our
 indigenous suburbs.

We scanned the horizon
like Arapaho braves
plotting Custer's Last Stand,
and just up the road , squadrons
of flying corn cobs gathered
to surround barn board basilicas.
Soon every 10 year old
was enjoined to gather round
and "See Rock City," "Put a Tiger in your
Tank!"
"Chew Copenhagen Tobacco"

When a D-day dawn of dandelion parachutes
crossed freshly sodded lawns,
and cat tail torches danced with us
around wooded hearted ravines

II.
Underneath painted columns at Memphis
mystery rites were once performed
midst introits for Isis, Osiris
their son Horus, and his brother Anubis.
Underneath Tyrian hashish plumes

draped in wreaths 'round midnight,
censers and cymbals bloom in lilac
majesty beyond our Hubbel telescope.
Pomegranate seeds and cinnamon
spice the nadir of my demitasse.
Censers and cymbals bloom lilac radiance,
as frail bean stalks of Camel smoke spiral
into flowery flights of tin ceiling.
  Fading beyond the Beal Street jail,
walking toward Jefferson Davis
Waterfront park, another blasted tourist
with clammy hands blends into the heat
of Memphis. Underneath painted columns
at Memphis, mystery rites
were once performed midst introits
for Isis, Osiris, their son Horus,
and his brother Anubis.

  III. jubilee
As yellow pines arched and wove
a lean-to over porous soil,
we skinned a mess of bullhead
one Sunday morning.
My uncle hammered their brains,
and spun out tightly curled souls.
My aunt then pushed her plier jaws
against the limp palate,
as lidless eyes tilted astride
her nickel plated pliers.
My uncle then etched confident lines
into their sepia rinds, and incised
white curves behind their hidden horns.
My aunt pulled flaps against his pulls,
gills flared red- like woodpecker heads.
Auntie nimbly flicked a serrated knife

under the meat, flaying roughly over
courses of noisy, carbuncle cartilage.
She slopped dishcloths of fish flank-
swished them in rosy water, and filled
her basin with treaded strips
that reminded me of softened sticks
of freshly unwrapped beachnut gum.
I rolled the pile of glistening remains
between sections of The Alpena News;
and delivered the lump beyond a screen
of linden trees.
Later, skittish shapes
congregated to snarl and laugh,
as smoke reclined over tar paper,
pine cones, and later on still-
a masked militia of fat raccoons
singing their midnight song,
as yellow pines arched and wove
a lean-to over porous soil.

IV. reverie
Men barked nonsense on Lunar hills,
deaf to the music of our moon.
When her glassine sands were pressed,
to transmit clips of harlequin white;
conquest illuminated the dome of night.
To understand why her ungodly face
appears to mourn; ask why
we strolled the lunar hills,
and danced upon her virgin humps,
with follicles, and fragile toes
encased in air conditioned boots.
And when each nerve is soothed enough
to see our silver mirror ebb and wax,
when spheres and hemispheres descend

to dream in undreamt volumes
deepened by a drum of tidal urge-
perhaps our sable voices will return
so that we sing, to sail
like drunken Greeks
through timeless stars, and stir
the rainless latitudes that sweep
to span the Sea of Tranquility.

V.
Better to misplace yesterday,
as rapiers of rain fall in escadrilles
like devils after pride-
to bathe a stoic neighborhood
in reams of squandered light;
while west to east is a hidden truth
perhaps, and thunderstorms coagulate
above birds of prey at sunset.
Thunderstorms enter to baptize homes-
blessed is the descent of a leaf,
dusty moths fluttering in emptiness,
and mushrooms, fiddleheads, fragments
of recollection gathered into stone
groves. Blessed is a golden curl in autumn,
as mourning is delivered by tumbling voices
-these are the voices of petals in a grave.
Blessed are the accompanists.
Blessed are tongue and larynx.
Banging my burled Milano onto dry land
today I produced a small pile of ashes
beneath the bowl, brown and burnt
against the dirt and singed earth.
I saw the first gulls
I had seen in months, while you
were making love somewhere else.

Autumn

Under the woven airs
of nimble words

chrysalides curve
into full blooded cocoons.

I may live decades
into jade old age

while erudite wings
remain dumbly furled.

Chrysalides curve
into full blooded cocoons

as faience inches
of summer elapse.

While erudite wings
remain dumbly furled

a cheap tapestry
of skyline unwraps.

As faience inches
of summer elapse,

the triumph of autumn
is self-assured.

A cheap tapestry
of skyline unwraps

while croci of my garden
born, collapse.

The triumph of autumn
is self-assured.

I may live decades
into jade old age

while croci of my garden
born, collapse

under the woven airs
of nimble words.

thank you dear reader

Acknowledgements

Poems or parts of poems within this collection have appeared the following publications:

print journals *Humanitas, Defined Providence, Portland Review, Nomad's Choir, The Vincent Brothers Review, Flying Horse, The Dry Creek Review, Poetry Motel, Tight, BlueLine, Plainsongs, Parnassus Literary Journal, Midwest Poetry Review, The Higginsville Reader, Voices International, Southern Poetry Review, Eccentricity, 12-gauge Review, 32 Pages, Obscure, Yomimono, The Poet's Edge, Illya's Honey, Kimera, Afterthoughts, Sierra Nevada College Review, Emu, Papier-Machete;*

Internet journals *Inter/face, The New Voice, Lexicon, Zuzu's Petals Quarterly, Poetry Cafe, World Wide Writing, Poetry Magazine, Immortali Et More, Thoth, Fresh Ink, Southern Ocean Review, Glossolalia, Brooklyn Poet, Anthem, Park & Read, A Room without Walls, Gravity, Recursive Angel, Ygdrasil, Gazet, Galapagos, 15 Credibility St., nrv8, Reflections from a Murky Pond, Pogonip, Slumgullion, The Astrophysicists Tango Partner Speaks, A Writer's Choice Literary Journal, Write On, Webgeist, Asili, Grepoetry, Black Street/Yellow Moon, Pauper, Night People, The Poetry Pavilion, Log Cabin Chronicles, New Works Review.*

The author is grateful to them all.

www.ingramcontent.com/pod-product-compliance
Lightning Source LLC
LaVergne TN
LVHW011412080426
835511LV00005B/498